PERCEPTION

D1279575

Also by Christina Pugh

Rotary
Restoration
Grains of the Voice

PERCEPTION

Christina Pugh

Four Way Books
Tribeca

Please direct all inquiries to:
Editorial Office
Four Way Books
POB 535, Village Station
New York, NY 10014
www.fourwaybooks.com

Library of Congress Cataloging-in-Publication Data

Names: Pugh, Christina, author.
Title: Perception / Christina Pugh.
Description: New York, NY : Four Way Books, [2017]
Identifiers: LCCN 2016034900 | ISBN 9781935536888 (pbk. : alk. paper)
Classification: LCC PS3616.U35 A6 2017 | DDC 811/.6--dc23
LC record available at https://lccn.loc.gov/2016034900

This book is manufactured in the United States of America and printed on acid-free paper.

Four Way Books is a not-for-profit literary press. We are grateful for the assistance
we receive from individual donors, public arts agencies, and private foundations.

This publication is made possible with public funds from the National Endowment for the Arts

and from the New York State Council on the Arts, a state agency.

We are a proud member of the Community of Literary Magazines and Presses.

Distributed by University Press of New England
One Court Street, Lebanon, NH 03766

for Rick

We make a dwelling in the evening air,
In which being there together is enough.

CONTENTS

—O remember

In your narrowing dark hours

That more things move

Than blood in the heart.

—Louise Bogan

The pious eye is reliable transportation.

—Donald Revell

1.

The aperture: the lens. The determinant ray. The conifer. The stripped-down. The lavish. The striped.

Occlusion. The numinous. The diamond. The horsefly. The firmament. Encaustic. The sea-bred. The trough.

The floater. The eye-pool. The lilac. The steamship. The Siamese. The rotifer. The mud bath. The crystal.

HAND-PRINT

Shake it   like a
Polaroid: the mind
draws the hand   as a
filament   of yaw—
gray gouache   pressed
as the   hectic
surface   of hibiscus:
furred *scabiosa,*   the
pincushion   flower

STAINED CALLA

Perimeter of
sunken trumpet:
smeared motes
of lily   throat
diminishing
in droplets
near the tendril-
hem   of the spathe

RAIN-SOAKED

Caladium's   a firebird

winged   from the silver-

fawn silt of its   foliage

surround: nesting in

feverish   fuchsia or

brimstone — Aramaic

blaze-   bush

legislates   in measures

SNAKE AMONG WEEDS

(on wallpaper)

Jade-starred	entity
lacing	embarking in
the self-spun	curve
of recursive	tailspin
tangled	in turquoise
underwater	bluegrass
stealth-steps	like arabesque
a form	slips eternal

SHOPWORN

Infinity they'd called it

in a faint   satin script:

dove-lit   stenciled

silhouette across   the door

inveterate   of wing-tip

beautify   the intent

swabbed   : near-razed-

up   quandary surround

LA BAGATELLE

in cursive yellow hung above

the shop   in the mall in the

seventies' west   An aureole

taper   Platonic

chandelier   *commedia*

(for Balanchine)

allegro   then marzipan

STAGE CLOUDS

1.

These fern   feather-shadows on my

sun-room   floor   drape

mobile as cirrus on the

dancers'   proscenium

2.

Her hand   is a beacon

scintilla at the

      lighthouse   :   follow it

      through ink   across the clarity

      of open sand

INSTRUMENTALITY

My watch-hand lights

solar-blue

in the   night

An arctic   ink-

stroke   startles

to the   stem

A WINDOW

In   air in

supplication

the four   ceramic

hands   rise

modeling a

serpentine   delft

along the   vellum

of the fingernail

THREE BLUE BUTTERFLIES

I.   MORPHO MENELAUS

Foiled acqua-

moiré wings the

butterfly's beauty-

mark hydraulic in its

purposes   his

hair's flame lifts

you snarls you

II.   MORPHO ACHILLES

Sea-bed in semaphore / an

eyepiece   wing-span

delft dye vat-dipped shingle

scintilla   :   truant

and acclimate   enfold

or infuriate: SOS:

Don't surround

Don't surround

yourself with yourself

III.   MORPHO RHETENOR HELENA

Neon heather sky-
lit bluer than moiré:

inseam of street
trash   lush mask-

contour   soul-
strait fungible

as raiment in the
crawlspace   radiating

amatory birds'
egg bulls-eye

THE PAINTING FLEW FROM THE WALL

When the twisters   were only

dark-   eyed incipience

it mustered   its gold its

mountainous its   vanishings

and breathed   at the

top of the   diving-tower

2.

The world is not what I think, but what I live through, said Merleau-Ponty, knowing that things both love and resist the fragile retina. Perspicuous arcs of disinterested phenomena: fireworks. Sultrier mirages over tar. Yet *no real landscape is itself unclear,* even when it hazes momentarily in my windshield: subtract me, and this juniper will porously reside. If I stay, let me labor for the industry of detail—the cross-hatched recesses; the scree or the muslin. A texture might be quick, but slowly learned. How to greet the entity?—partially, musically: be muscular. At times, I want to clasp it in the long arms of metaphor.

IMMERSION

That   butterfly had

carried   a   night

upon its   wings:

can you   try

then to   tip

bright   Venus

to your   face

like a   page

ANGLE OF A LANDSCAPE

Angle in the prairie   see the
cloud-dial   riven gold

pendulum, you're turning home
the sky   wets its quill

SIERRA NEVADA

An inroad   of diamond

fretwork   in the cliff-side

asked to be   secret its

open-work   in all our eyes

WINGAERSHEEK BEACH

Turner   could try it the

lighthouse   shriven pearl

the scumbling   immersive

cloud a   dog's   paws

carpeting the   sand in   coronas

ON METAPHOR

A suspension

bridge   now

rises from

the road   or

doesn't it

resolve   into

the   waist

of a violin   its

bridge under

strings   Such

transport

rectitude

imminent

intangible

A TWIG OF EVIDENCE

Amid Green—

A corkscrew   branch

denuded   of leaves :

furrowing   in arteries

it   lists   like a twister

of structure

CLOUDED GLASS

(Christopher Dresser)

Soon to be poured, what

can't conserve in beakers or

experiments to dam the drear

rills of cognition: to pour

as museum pieces pouring

nothing but some negative

theology:: the convex

swoon in the billowed

lip of the Dresser vase

BURLAP

Cochineal stain clean-
framed in the Martinez
hacienda

A nectar   a tincture
some peony
in burlap   an
evidential   stirring of the
rose(st) magenta

the never-
evanescence
when a wheel

ARCHIVAL SLIP

(Emily Dickinson)

Letters fleet

and half-

evasive *My first*

My first The third

proto-word is

inchoate as

calligraphy,

champagne

bubbles I could

not read in

Arabic—it might

be *Jasmine,*

what they

call on the street:

siren or dog-star

dressy in leaves

PINK QUILL

Tillandsia cyanea Bromeliaceae

Arcing plum-

blue   within a

cold   front

of gray :   these

three   prehensile

petals   tendril,

germinate   the

implement

LUNAR LIVING

... like women feeling for the smoothness of yard-goods.
—Elizabeth Bishop

A farming of

beams, this

cultivar of

hornbeam or

girl-cantilever

or viridian

chanteuse: taffeta

crushed at the

sackcloth

abutment—

smooth

it   garner it

finger it

HAT-RACK

Forest- sequined

beanie   with a drifting

of net   Or in points:

diamonded   cartography

for foreheads   carnation

in velvet   the sleet-

wilt of orchids   hydrangea

A LINTEL

Terra-cotta wet

with the motions

of traffic

A rotary deep

within an ozone

layer   Or the

necklacing of

taillights as I

land above the river

3.

Something I learned about *agape* when I was young: the *Iliad* tells
us fellow-feeling is finite in communities. Brotherly love becomes a
number that has to be divided among persons—so if you're too kind to
others, that might explain your neighbor's graft. I sometimes wonder if
perception is the same; if the quantity of percepts, or our trove of eidetic
things, is not limitless but rather constant: the measure, say, of a sunlit
field. So if we dip like deep-sea divers to the world, we'll have to use a
purse-seine to sieve our sense impressions. We're hoarding the image
at our peril. That bluest scilla smeared by a finger writing in the grass?
Endangered. Poetry's work is not to ravish, but diminish.

SWEAT

(Elephant-ear)

The tremolo

globe of the

Colocasia's tear

gems at the

leaf-tip then wells,

precipitous

PAPERWEIGHT

Genius loci: folds
of   nymphaea
blushing   in a
planetary   foliage

VIOLENCE

(Kiki Smith)

This sleeping   beauty's

white   on white:

the tundra   of her

forehead's   plaster;

almond   holes

replace her   eyes

CORPS DE BALLET

A raft of tulle hovers

over feet in *croisé:*

skirts levitated under

arms' undulating

stems in photographic

white-life : twilit

mast mi-creature

or marine

AQUARIUM

Are you noticing the range

of motion in the skate

the sea turtle furrowing

the water as she fans

TWOMBLY'S PEONIES

There are deep   atomic clouds

in *rain-green*   *Oregon*   the

rain has   rained away the

stems the   leaves   the

haiku   penciled   in to

fasten   down the gas

BOTANY

The botanical element is a living plant which overgrows
the dead and rigid scaffolding of the letter.
            —Otto Pacht, *Book Illumination in the Middle Ages*

Thus   I am

surprised   that the

tendrils growing from the

precipice-drop atop the

C   aren't green

but a   vintner's Midas-

generous who

sways   from mimesis

LES FLEURS DU MAL

The eye the   eye

rhymes   black-blood

irises   on sky

TWOMBLY'S PEONIES (II)

a blood-loop   *sans serif*

or polyps   as the petals

foliate the   texture

of tumors   over gold

RADIO MARIGOLD

Impazzito   di luce   cloven
by light   or the   site   of the
orange   crushed   so dreadlock
rays are   marine   band waves
and your   eyes my eyes are
grazing the   frequency

GLENN GOULD

The marrow's

matchstick   the

sharp of the

elbow   the

skull   inclining

over   hammers

over   keys

A WING

Fame: the Corinthian   mosaic on

a dragonfly   or dim

racketeering   of the commoner   moth

WHAT OUTLINES OR WHAT FADES AWAY

the left

hand the writing

hand the pencil

pressing firm

to form a

muscle tendon

sinew; the right

hand ephemeral

as steam within

the graphite

4.

They can x-ray your retina now. The doctor took the picture, then
swiveled her monitor to show me the image. It looked like the tundra,
or a desert with a little dip. Chalk plains, no grasses. And a hardwood
grain, as in old documentaries. If you lived there, you'd be very alone—
more alone than Wyoming in winter. But I don't live in a landscape like
that. Or I do: there's a sanctity in everything impersonal.

PORCUPINE WASH

(a photograph by Daniel Kukla)

here   amid tumbleweed

so hoary   in the darkness

and the   calcinate

fingers   of desert-

thriving   coral:

a square   pricked by

constellations

set   upon an easel

to mirror   a neighboring

graft   of the real

METHOD

Can the retina

glean can it

willow (we

select): this

marble's

a mirror

of the bluish

in my

eye-pool

BEARDED IRIS

In the   Sheridan

garden   they are

mantled   in hues in

luxe in   conspicuous

auricular   shifts

THE NEST

twine   and birch bark

thicket   or welt

pied   egg cleaned

from a   jag   in its

shell: hide this

now behind an

increment

of iron   fence

URBAN

The near wall

cracks as if woolen

underneath: in the

stained glass

studio, Joseph's

robe folds milky,

impervious—a

cross atop the

scroll rose-lit

MOSAIC

Ocean   (or mountainous)

cut within the banister

Vesuvian the   thumbprint

hemmed by   isosceles

in circles

PHONING IN THE SWALLOWTAIL

aphonic   but limning

a fingerling   screen — the

motion of the   snapping

cell made   oak leaves

lusher less bristled   fresher

that triangle   of wing a

goldener   mean

THE STONE

This one   tattooed by

Superior's waves   if a

snake had   slid across

to ink   some faint and

sinewy   stripe to   bisect

sheets of   less-than-

incandescent   light

SEA GOOSEBERRY

trailing   its opal lamp

its   pare-strand

of angel   hair it

flickers   a microscopic

seaward   marquis

FRAMED DRAGONFLY

The wings are   nearly

nothing   some filament

from baby's   brush

The wing   thus

porthole   to the leaf

5.

I fractured my ankle near a wildflower preserve here in northern Illinois.
I had fallen on my way to the bee balm growing in the field.

I'd wanted open air: to see a corner of the prairie at very close range.

And an infinitesimal tattering of bee balm in the grass.

But my talus bone had shattered. I'd have to go inside—to digital
gardens with their indistinct leaves. Is perception less real, when less
immediate? I thought so at first. But then, who's to choose? This crewel-
work on my comforter shows no less design than the petals in the field.
And small things shine like prisms in the distance.

A SMALLER PURPLE

Small   like the bee's
balm   remembered
in the field — a tatter
in the blossom   and
the hue   faded
eastward: — deep

sips   missing
from the   beveled
glass that   constitutes
our   loved
color, violet

FIREFLIES FROM A DISTANCE

(The Shut-In)

Even from my   window

the gold   lights   longer

the sky now   building

a blue   ridge against

the pine   the north

shale layer   suffusing

ever   fainter

LANTERN

when gray   clouds shade

the half- moon lantern

it bathes   their edges it

kindles   their   perimeter

so gray will   elongate

north   northwest as

cumulous   thins the

dark   becomes the

pith   of the dark

PURLING FOUNTAIN

would it   please you again

if I were to   describe it well

the soft   lucid burble

in a pine-   stained

basin the   line of a

poem that's   chiseling

invisible   to those

who stir   above

APRIL

6 pm   light: near-
ravishing   from shadow:
stealing   over   beaded
buds on   this   slender
birch   branch

INSTRUMENTALITY (II)

(Lenovo)

it impersonates   a book it's

shimmering   the crescent

phase   : back to

work and it's   dark

o' the moon

LOST BINOCULARS

the commoner   gull

is a   showering of   sun

not the   crane the

pelican   thinning

in the   distance

THE SMALLEST

path in the   arboretum

eye-beam   an artery

a shock of   Russian sage

that   lilacs into

nothingness   the yellow

vetch   the blackberry

the torn   ruined Susan

TERRITORY

I traded a firmament

for waters   smote with

continents for   form for

a strip-seam   riveting

the ocean

6.

I was showing you the house on the shore where we'd live together. I had just bought the property and was proud: we'd always wanted to live on the ocean. Then you pointed to something in the distance—a thin waterfall set northeasterly in our field of view. I hadn't noticed it when I bought the house. But you showed it to me knowingly, without surprise or fanfare.

It was something like the snapshot I keep from years ago: dog days in Washington state, riding with you in the Saturn on the highway. The A/C was broken. But I felt a shock of sudden cool—you'd turned off the road at a forest preserve. We walked down a path there, following the pines to the lull and lucid droplets of a hidden waterfall—it could have been Bogan's fountain *flinging diamond water.* In gratitude, I took the picture. Why do I display it after all these years? Nothing extraordinary happened to us there. But these are the instants I'm learning to call *memory.*

LITTLE AS A DAFFODIL:

What's suited then to fill

the ravenous

pupil of the mind's

little eye: what

butters

and frills   what

pixellates, thickening

a fierce(st)
remembrance

STAYS

recall chiffon   skirts

that billow   over grates—

so the wind   flips   webs

of   fir-green   bracts,

fingering   wiring that

anchors the   panicles   my

Queen's   dense lace

BLACK BRA

Naught to fill :

a closed

book: almanac

unhooked—

corvine silken

epistle to

an evening

PEACHES

Can it   be a

miracle   (or only

for me)   the rose-

steeped-sunset -   flawed

circularity   my lip

against its   softness

the runnel   of its wet

LA BAGATELLE (II)

Remember   the crinkle

of stars around your

neck the   clasp

the   fumble

of dressing   in the night

HINDSIGHT

we were   watching

your son   chase the

floating feral   milkweed

tuft   aloft   in the

condo's dusk: that

softer   spider   we

too once   took

for a   creature

PAPERWEIGHT (II)

These   swans in

convocation

at the stillest

point   of the

labyrinth's glass . . .

you and I we'd

walked it   together,

touched   the fiery

hibiscus at the

center   and the

golden   Gate

amid the mist

HELLENIC

(He Asked:)

could you   make   of your

body   a single   ear:...

and   then her

head   rose   imperial-

white more   richly

robed than it   had

ever been   O how

could I   lose what

never   was

SHE ASKED

What's the place that knows?

I traced inside the heart-

beat but ended in the

brain pan: penciled

moths were swarming

open, laboring

the snow

CALL THE SOUL

Not just   a flame
but a   foliate
flame: never
concentric   nor rippled-
meteoric   but
haptic   tactical
retinal   a breadbox

7.

In the end, the problem of the redwoods is a problem of scale. How can I understand a body that exceeds my eye so utterly? Like Psyche, I'm entering cathedrals I must never see: the redwoods' lowest branches touch the clouds. But I can't help myself—I still see trees in the human way. Every spring, a Callery pear tree used to drape white blossoms in our third-floor window: first panicle, then leaf to leaf, caught in that transparency for all my contemplation. The pear's early flowers were threaded with green on the day the city cut it down. A worker left me a round from the trunk. It was smooth, almost polished—I saw that he'd sanded it with something like love. In my empty window now, an old line stays: *let the sky be a lilac brought close to the eye.*

LAST

(As the verb)   as a

tulip   blade

saffrons   the rapier

Pear-tree   leafing

in your back-crop

of blossom: preserve

that   whiteness

still my sight

PROXIMATE

> I'll lie here and learn
> How, over their ground,
> Trees make a long shadow
> And a light sound.
> —Louise Bogan

Some leaves   cut

star-shaped   outlines

dappling the   others

the oak   thus

speaking

to itself   in sun

is it too   much to call

darkness   propinquity

a lance a   chisel

to imprint   what's

intricate   what hews

so   airily

from structure   Is darkness

then   perimeter

Is light

DREAM GLANCE

The trunks'   slow

glimmer   as sherry

in the   glass

floating   branchless

où flotte la

blanche   Ophélia

ENDING EDEN

(Kiki Smith)

Here is the stone   hand

orbiting the   sheen

of the sea-   green

fruit its   halo a

hunger her   hand's

near-arc   thus

fluttering   good-bye

A SHAPELESS FRIEND

parched   and ethereal—

gaseous   thus colorless

remorse   less traveled or

the scavenger   dead: our

shapely   acquaintances

less intimate   than   you

LOST FRANKLINIA

(An extinct flower)

Early to bed, early to rise

lost to us:	poor
Richard's	aphoristic
life—or	glimmered
now as	neuroscience,
petals	driven white

FINIS

Look at the spent

anemone,   she said—

the   water-

sugar   petals

must have

fallen   from

her   coin-purse

SCINTILLA

And yet   still it *is*

there the   metaphor

in voiceless   gleam the

wind-   water-   strider

near   so numinous the

plash and   swath

of the   surfaces

SUMMER'S END

You   know I'd

grown   accustomed

to the pink-   seamed

veins   of *Caladium*

fire the   mirror

of sky-shell   shined

across my   table

Some things I overlooked, and some I could not find.

Let the crystal clasp them

When you drink your wine, in autumn.

—Louise Bogan

NOTES

"Shake it like a Polaroid" is taken from "Hey Ya!," written by André 3000.

"Don't surround yourself with yourself" is taken from "I've Seen All Good People," written by Jon Anderson and Chris Squire.

In "Twombly's Peonies," the phrase "rain-green Oregon" is taken from Olga Broumas's "sometimes, as a child," in *Beginning with O*. "The sky be a lilac brought close to the eye" is taken from *Black Holes, Black Stockings*, by Olga Broumas and Jane Miller. Other poems contain italicized lines, sometimes slightly paraphrased, from the work of Arthur Rimbaud and Eugenio Montale.

Several poems' titles are phrases, or partial phrases, taken from the poetry of Emily Dickinson—as discrete instances of "seeing," both concrete and abstract. "A Wing" is taken from Dickinson's #1788; "Angle of a Landscape" is taken from #578; "A Twig of Evidence" is taken from #373; "A Smaller Purple" from #281; "Territory" from #568; "Little as a Daffodil" from #361; and "A Shapeless Friend" from #679. "Burlap" and "Archival Slip" are also partially inspired by Dickinson texts, the latter referring to one of Dickinson's notes on display at the New York Botanical Garden in the summer of 2010.

In "Dream Glance," the phrase "sherry / in the glass" is taken from Dickinson's letter #268 (July 1862) to Thomas Wentworth Higginson, in which she describes "my eyes, like the Sherry in the Glass, that the Guest leaves—"

ACKNOWLEDGMENTS

Grateful acknowledgment is made to the editors of the following publications, in which some of these poems have appeared or are forthcoming:

Barrow Street, Birmingham Poetry Review, Colorado Review, The Economy, Field, Fifth Wednesday, Jet Fuel Review, Ocean State Review, Plume, Plume Anthology 5, Poetry Northwest, and *Poetry Quarterly.*

My sincere thanks to the Ragdale Foundation for residencies in which some of these poems were written, and warm thanks in particular to the Ragdale residents of April and May, 2013. I am also grateful to the University of Illinois at Chicago for providing me a sabbatical in which to complete this book, and to Bruce Bennett for reading and encouraging early versions of some of these poems. Heartfelt thanks to my mother, Sybil Pugh; my sister, Wendy Jones; and my father, Walter Pugh. Though he did not live to see the book's publication, his memory and spirit infuse these pages—as does my gratitude to him. Endless thanks and love to my husband, Rick DelVisco. My thanks also to Lisa Petrie and Phillis Levin; and to Martha Rhodes, Ryan Murphy, and Four Way Books.

Christina Pugh is the author of three previous books of poems: *Grains of the Voice* (Northwestern University Press, 2013), *Restoration* (Northwestern University Press, 2008), and *Rotary* (Word Press, 2004), which received the Word Press First Book Prize. Her poems have appeared in *The Atlantic, The Kenyon Review, Poetry, Ploughshares,* and many other periodicals. She was awarded a John Simon Guggenheim Fellowship in poetry for 2015-2016 and a Bogliasco Foundation Fellowship in 2016. Her previous awards have included the Lucille Medwick Award from the Poetry Society of America, a poetry fellowship from the Illinois Arts Council, and the Grolier Poetry Prize. Her essays have appeared in *The Cambridge Companion to Poetry Since 1945, The Emily Dickinson Journal, Literary Imagination,* and *Poetry,* among other publications. She is a professor in the Program for Writers at the University of Illinois at Chicago, and consulting editor for *Poetry.*

Publication of this book was made possible by grants and donations. We are also grateful to those individuals who participated in our 2016 Build a Book Program. They are:

Anonymous (8), Evan Archer, Sally Ball, Jan Bender-Zanoni, Zeke Berman, Kristina Bicher, Carol Blum, Lee Briccetti, Deirdre Brill, Anthony Cappo, Carla & Steven Carlson, Maxwell Dana, Machi Davis, Monica Ferrell, Martha Webster & Robert Fuentes, Dorothy Goldman, Lauri Grossman, Steven Haas, Mary Heilner, Henry Israeili, Christopher Kempf, David Lee, Jen Levitt, Howard Levy, Owen Lewis, Paul Lisicky, Katie Longofono, Cynthia Lowen, Louise Mathias, Nathan McClain, Gregory McDonald, Britt Melewski, Kamilah Moon, Carolyn Murdoch, Tracey Orick, Zachary Pace, Gregory Pardlo, Allyson Paty, Marcia & Chris Pelletiere, Eileen Pollack, Barbara Preminger, Kevin Prufer, Peter & Jill Schireson, Roni & Richard Schotter, Soraya Shalforoosh, Peggy Shinner, James Snyder & Krista Fragos, Megan Staffel, Marjorie & Lew Tesser, Susan Walton, Calvin Wei, Abigail Wender, Allison Benis White, and Monica Youn.